~ FIRST GREEK MYTHS ~
ARION THE DOLPHIN BOY

For Pamela Fluke
S.P.
To all my boys
J.L.

ORCHARD BOOKS
338 Euston Road, London NW1 3BH
Orchard Books Australia
Level 17/207 Kent Street, Sydney NSW 2000
This text was first published in the form of a gift collection
called *First Greek Myths* by Orchard Books in 2003
This edition first published in hardback by Orchard Books in 2008
First paperback publication in 2009
Text © Saviour Pirotta 2008
Cover illustrations © Jan Lewis 2008
Inside illustrations © Jan Lewis 2008
The rights of Saviour Pirotta to be identified as the author and
of Jan Lewis to be identified as the illustrator of this work
have been asserted by them in accordance with the
Copyright, Designs and Patents Act, 1988.
A CIP catalogue record for this book is available from the British Library.
ISBN 978 1 84616 474 3 (hardback)
ISBN 978 1 84616 772 0 (paperback)
1 3 5 7 9 10 8 6 4 2 (hardback)
1 3 5 7 9 10 8 6 4 2 (paperback)
Orchard Books is a division of Hachette Children's Books,
an Hachette Livre UK company.
Printed in China

www.orchardbooks.co.uk

~ FIRST GREEK MYTHS ~
ARION THE DOLPHIN BOY

BY SAVIOUR PIROTTA
ILLUSTRATED BY JAN LEWIS

ORCHARD BOOKS

~ CAST LIST ~

ARION
(Ar-y-on)

THE KING

There was once a great poet called Arion. He was a shy young man and he liked it best when he was at home, writing poems and playing sweet music on his harp.

But Arion was the greatest poet in the world and rich kings from far-off lands wanted him to write special poems just for them. They showered him with fabulous gifts.

After one visit to a prince, Arion
was on his way home on a small
ship. He had been given a chest
of jewels. Whatever would he do
with it all?

Arion took out his harp and
started to play a happy song.

The sailors huddled together
and muttered. "Let's steal his
treasure and throw him
overboard," suggested one.

"We could just tell our king that he couldn't resist living in the other king's magnificent palace so he stayed behind," said another.

Arion looked up from his harp as the sailors gathered around him. "Would you like to hear another song?" he asked.

"No, what we really want is your treasure!" the captain bellowed. He took out a knife.

"Please," Arion begged. "Don't kill me. You can have my treasure. I don't want it – take it all."

"You'd report us to the king as soon as we got back home," said the captain, pointing his knife at Arion's throat. "No, we will have to feed you to the sharks!"

"At least let me sing one last song," said Arion, trembling with fear.

"All right," agreed the captain. "But make it quick."

Arion started playing again. As he played, dolphins and seagulls gathered round to listen.

"Let's get this over and done with," the captain said as he reached out and pushed Arion off the deck.

"Aaaaagh! HELP!" cried Arion.
He tried to stay afloat in the
waves, but he couldn't swim.

Just then, a dolphin pushed
gently against Arion's harp and
lifted him out of the water. He
had been rescued!

Happily, Arion picked up his harp
and began playing a cheerful song.
He didn't stop until the dolphin
had taken him all the way home.

"Arion!" cried his king. "Welcome back! But how did you get here? Where is your ship? And where are the other sailors?"

Arion explained everything that
had happened.

A few days later, Arion's
ship arrived.

As soon as the sailors were back
on dry land, the king came to
greet them. He asked them where
the famous poet was.

23

"He decided to stay behind," said the captain.

"When do you think he will return?" asked the king, looking the captain straight in the eye.

"Perhaps he will stay there for ever," the sailors shrugged.

In the water behind them a dolphin cawed. It sounded as though he were laughing.

The sailors spun round and
their faces turned a ghostly white.
There was Arion!

"How did he get here?" the captain said, panicking. "We begged him to come back. Didn't we, lads?"

All the other sailors nodded in
agreement, but the king was
not fooled.

"You are liars," he said, "and you shall be punished. Take them to a desert island and leave them there," he ordered the guards.

The kind dolphin who rescued Arion was looked after by the people of the kingdom until he died.

Then the gods turned the dolphin into a cluster of bright stars to help guide travellers back home.

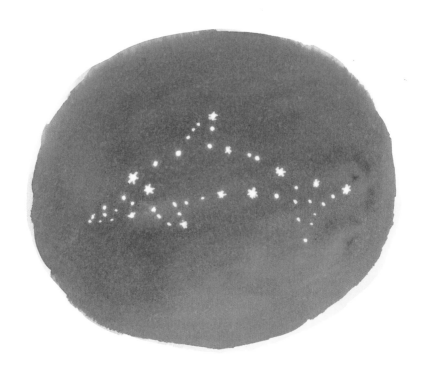

And as for the treasure...well,
Arion let the sailors keep that.
But what use are gold and jewels
on a desert island?

~ FIRST GREEK MYTHS ~
ARION, THE DOLPHIN BOY

BY SAVIOUR PIROTTA ~ ILLUSTRATED BY JAN LEWIS

And enjoy a little magic with these First Fairy Tales:

First Greek Myths and First Fairy Tales are available from all
good bookshops, or can be ordered direct from the publisher:
Orchard Books, PO BOX 29, Douglas IM99 1BQ
Credit card orders please telephone 01624 836000
or fax 01624 837033
or e-mail: bookshop@enterprise.net for details.

To order please quote title, author and ISBN
and your full name and address.
Cheques and postal orders should be
made payable to 'Bookpost plc'.
Postage and packing is FREE within the UK
(overseas customers should add £1.00 per book).

Prices and availability are subject to change.